When Leaders Leave
A New Perspective on Leadership Change

Priscilla Rosenwald
Lesley Mallow Wendell

Published by Marketshift, Inc.,
Philadelphia, Pennsylvania.

Published by MarketShift, Inc.
833 N. 28th Street
Philadelphia, PA 19130

Printed in the United States of America
12 11 10 09 08 07 06 05 04 03 02 01

Rosenwald, Priscilla; Wendell, Lesley Mallow
When Leaders Leave
ISBN – 978-0-9895813-0-1
1. Nonprofit business 2. Leadership transition
3. Change management

This book is available at special discounts for bulk purchases
in the United States by corporations, institutions and other
organizations. For more information please
contact: myoung@marketshift.net.

For more information about leadership transition,
go to transitionworks.com.

Dedication

Writing this book has been a creative process like no other. Thank you, Priscilla, for convincing me to come along for the journey. And to Gary, Ben and Maddy, thank you for being a constant wellspring of support for all my professional endeavors.—Lesley Mallow Wendell

I dedicate this book to my enthusiastic supporters, Shira Haaz and Sharla Floyd, for their inspiration, imagination and ingenuity. This has been an amazing journey. My deep gratitude to Lesley for her thoughtful partnership.
— Priscilla Rosenwald

Acknowledgements

We dedicate this book to each and every one of our dynamic clients who have given us this window into the challenges of managing and surviving a leadership change. You have inspired us to think more expansively and share our learning broadly in the hope that nonprofits everywhere can benefit from your experiences.

Our work has informed our practice and provided many examples that underscore our experiences and learning. The cases included in *When Leaders Leave* are based on real-life situations, which we share with the utmost discretion and respect for our clients' confidentiality.

We also pay tribute to our editor, Miki Young, whose creativity and stewardship made this book a reality.

Contents

— Introduction —

Change is constant. And a change in leadership is inevitable. That's true even when that leader is the founder who passionately embraced a societal need, brought together bright and promising people to think about solutions, and created the organization. At some time, at some point, that founder/leader will move on.

This book is about a change in leadership, which often strikes fear at the very heart of an organization. It can throw the board, staff and leadership into turmoil. In fact, people go to great lengths to avoid disrupting the status quo. Sometimes, they even stay in bad relationships because it seems like a more palatable option. If we are overwhelmed by the fear of new leadership and we try to hold onto the way it's always been, we expend a lot of energy resisting change. Successful organizations have the stability and the resiliency to respond to changes in both their internal and external environments.

Change in leadership is, indeed, a painful thought. But avoiding it or pretending that it won't happen could put the organization in long-term jeopardy. What is most important is that the facts are faced and parameters put in place to ensure the organization will continue to thrive and stand on its own without the current leadership. Planning for change is critical because it ensures that the organization's leadership can continue to address its mission in positive ways.

Planning ahead and thinking through that potential change in leadership for the chief executive and, sometimes, for the board chair, is actually a series of three processes that support the organization's overall strength and development: leadership legacy planning, succession planning and transition planning.

These distinct processes are used to effectively address a change in leadership. Some of these happen concurrently, some are continual, and some occur at a specific time during a leadership change event.

Leadership legacy planning. This is the biggest landscape in which to view the inevitability of leadership transition. It is an ongoing process that should occur *even if the organization is not planning on a leadership change.* It requires the leadership to align the legacy of the executive director and the organization and to take the steps to resolve any conflict between the two. This ensures viability beyond the involvement of the founder or long-term leader.

Succession planning. This plan is a strategic overview of the steps necessary to ensure the organization's capacity to thrive when the leader leaves. The focus is on how the organization will develop resiliency and strengthen the leadership talent. The emergency succession plan will detail the actions to be taken under various scenarios, such as an unplanned emergency leave or a planned departure with long-term notice. Optimally, the succession plan will be reviewed yearly, in conjunction with the strategic plan.

Transition planning. This plan only occurs once the leader has identified that he or she is planning to move on, regardless of whether it will be an immediate exit or a longer process. It is an active plan that identifies the steps to assess the organization's strengths, evaluate the opportunity, plan the search and hire, and determine the most effective way to support the current leader's leaving and the new leader's arrival and on-boarding.

Leadership legacy planning assures the organization's ability to survive and thrive. This focus is actually part of an important ongoing process in which the organization periodically assesses its vision based on the reality of current needs, and refines its optimal path for growth. This process also provides a roadmap to ensure that all levels of leadership are aligned with the same focus.

An active leadership legacy plan lays the foundation for a healthy organization to:

- realistically know its strengths and weaknesses.
- attract, retain and develop robust talent.

- have a high-functioning board.
- develop a strong management team.
- pursue innovation and resiliency.
- stay on course with its mission.

With advanced leadership leadership legacy planning, the organization will survive a leadership transition and actually thrive because of the reflection inherent in the process and the diverse thinking and energy brought by a new CEO.

The opportunities abound. Every organization has the potential to go through a leadership change and emerge with strength. The transition provides a unique occasion for the organization to manage change by establishing sound leadership practices and creating an environment of resiliency.

When Leaders Leave is a how-to book with essential tools for the Board and the CEO to plan for that inevitable transition, avoid pitfalls, and smooth out the path. It can help board chairs who are thinking about leadership legacy and succession planning, foundations who are asking organizations to look at the distant horizon, and CEOs who know that five years down the road there will be other challenges calling.

We are living in times of change. In the nonprofit sector, there is considerable leadership transition among boards and executive directors as the boomers move on and the next generation comes into the lead. Accepting leadership change as inevitable can be the engine that fuels the resiliency and agility an organization needs to thrive.

Because change is the only constant we can count on, we all need to embrace it and figure out how to use it in our favor so that we can help our organizations grow and evolve. Here's what we know.

Leaders leave. Whether it's a founder leader with beginning thoughts about retirement, a new generation leader just starting her planned five-year run, or a transition in board leadership, organizations are always in flux somewhere on the continuum of leadership transition.

Leadership change is a challenge. Leadership change is not simple. It impacts every employee, board member and stakeholder in the organization. Anticipating that challenge in advance ultimately smoothes out the process and prepares the organization for a successful transition and integration of new leadership.

Leadership change is opportunity. Knowing that change is inevitable opens the doorway to new thinking about how an organization and its leaders can positively impact the mission. When the environment supports a mantra of continual growth, new directions will evolve. Seeing change as opportunity means that management always has an eye toward long-term growth and development for the individual *and* for the organization.

Leadership legacy planning allows organizations to maintain a strategic view and incorporate essential tools that can identify when change is needed. This strategic leadership planning should be board-driven, yet collaborative with senior leaders and proactively create a process that supports growth, finds optimal leadership talent, and establishes a path to fluently incorporate new leadership.

There are seven steps to get your organization to the place where it can effectively manage change:

1. **Start where you are.** Know how the organization is currently positioned for change. Objectively evaluate the organization's strengths and challenges and determine the best way to embrace change.
2. **Align the legacies.** Understand where the organization is in its development *and* where the CEO is. Know where the organization must go to stay relevant in achieving its mission. Understand the blend of responsibility between the board and the CEO for determining where the leader's legacy and the organization's legacy intersect.
3. **Help the leader find his or her way.** It's important that true alignment exist between the founder's personal/professional goals and objectives and the direction of the organization. This requires

positive, honest conversation that respects the needs of both the organization and the individual.

4. **Plan for success. Plan for succession.** Focus on growing leaders and building a better board. Value and strengthen the organization's talent and identify the strengths of staff and board members who can be nurtured and developed.

5. **Kickstart the leadership transition.** Support the outgoing leader in making positive plans for his exit. Identify the necessary steps to support both organizational sustainability and the leader.

6. **Reach for the sky.** Find a leader who will match the forward-thinking evolution of the organization. Or determine that it is best to hold off the search and choose an interim director.

7. **Smooth sailing.** Create a smooth transition that will take a new leader through the on-boarding period.

By addressing leadership legacy planning head-on, organizations take charge of their changing circumstances rather than become overwhelmed by them, and move forward to a positive new era.

— Chapter One —
Start Where You Are

Well-led organizations have a culture that easily adapts to change. The fact is that change is continual. There are new hires, refined strategic goals and new partnerships. Many organizations do not adapt easily to these changes and, instead, develop a stance that they are just fine the way they are until faced with a "major change event" such as a leadership transition.

The best way to prepare for change is to start before it happens. The first step is to realistically assess how the organization responds to change. Does it approach change head on? Does it communicate openly and seriously invite input from all interested stakeholders? Does it proactively review potential challenges? And does it align expectations and rewards?

Pema Chodron, a notable American figure in Tibetan Buddhism, wrote a book entitled *Start Where You Are,*[1] and the advice is particularly appropriate here. To effectively lay a solid foundation with which to manage change, organizations need to know their starting point.

Using the following Change Readiness Survey, an organization can begin to see how it views and manages change. The results of the survey will surface many of the challenges, and provide insights into how to proactively address them. The survey can be used to initiate a creative and productive conversation about how to prepare for and manage change.

---

1 Chodron, Pema. *Start Where You Are: A Guide to Compassionate Living.* Shambala Press, 2001.

Change Readiness Survey

Answer each question by using the following scale:

1 = Strongly Disagree   2 = Disagree   3 = Not Sure 4 = Agree   5 = Strongly Agree

a. When Board leadership talks about change, they provide a clear vision for what the future looks like. _____

b. Organizational leadership communicates the rationale behind significant proposed change. _____

c. Staff and stakeholders are actively involved in planning for change and helping to shape the desired future. _____

d. Board, leadership and senior staff consistently demonstrate support for important changes. _____

e. Board, leadership and staff are able to identify potential obstacles to implementing change. _____

f. Communication channels are open and allow for continuous feedback and information sharing by board, staff and stakeholders. _____

g. Board and staff leadership actively welcome input from employees concerning challenges, expectations and innovations relative to the proposed changes. _____

h. New expectations and standards that accompany change are clearly communicated; desired actions are positively reinforced. _____

Change Readiness Survey continued

1 = Strongly Disagree 2 = Disagree 3 = Not Sure
4 = Agree 5 = Strongly Agree

i. Board, leadership and staff are equipped with the skills, knowledge and competencies required to make the changes work. _____

j. Staff receives regular feedback about how well they are meeting changing expectations. _____

k. The organization provides recognition (through celebrations, rewards or other acknowledgement) when key benchmarks in the change process are reached. _____

l. The organization leads, manages and supports change in an effective, motivating manner. _____

Total Score _____

Change Acceptance Continuum

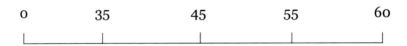

| 0 | 35 | 45 | 55 | 60 |

Rejects Change   **Embraces Change**

A score of 55 – 60   **The organization effectively manages change.**

A score of 45 – 54   **Some aspects of change need to be managed better by the organization. Review the questions to see where the strengths and weaknesses lie and begin discussions.**

A score of 35 – 44   **You should take immediate action to strengthen your change management process. Set up a taskforce to prioritize as follows: a) those challenges which have the most negative impact and can be most easily changed; b) those challenges which have the most negative impact and will take the most effort to change. Create a strategic action plan for each category.**

A score below 35   **Your organization will struggle to implement and sustain change. Consider calling in an outside objective partner to help deepen your analysis and recommend potential actions.**

Storm Cloud: Because they are focused on managing a transition at the top of the organization, boards often forget the impact of leadership change on staff.

It will be important to understand where the organization lies on the Change Acceptance Continuum to develop effective strategies that address specific challenges and enable forward movement through the change process.

Rose Kennedy, President of the Kennedy Group and a leading expert on managing change, has created a useful model that addresses four stages of change; the primary issues associated with each; observable behaviors; costs to the organization; outcomes and specific actions leaders can take to address them. This model appears, with permission from the author, in the Appendix, page (A).

Well-led organizations are prepared for long-term leadership changes. They often use change to leverage substantial growth. These organizations flourish because they know it is important to be able to answer the question of what would happen if the chief executive received a "can't turn it down opportunity" that required her to leave in the next month? These are the same organizations which insist that every strategic plan includes a succession plan. This ensures that the organization is prepared to function effectively during a three-to-six month absence of the chief executive.

Illumination: Engaging the staff in conversations where they can provide input and express concerns can go a long way to ensure stability and sustainability through the process.

Storm Cloud: The board of an organization, with a charismatic leader who effectively raises money and visibility, may coast or, even worse, "put their heads in the sand." The board may defer or abdicate responsibility for ongoing assessment, performance management and a strong strategic planning process.

Organizations that are not contemplating a change in leadership can become complacent, especially in the areas of organizational effectiveness and leadership development. Some believe a focus on leadership development is too expensive or unnecessary because the current leadership has demonstrated long-term stability, up to this point.

Advanced Planning

A Philadelphia-based education think tank, co-led for decades by founders, initiated the transition management process two years in advance of their planned departure. The board began to evolve from being founder-led and started to proactively incorporate good governance practices. The staff engaged in change management activities and processes to increase their understanding and acceptance of how the organization might transform. By the time the founders left their roles, a dynamic new chief executive was able to lead the organization through growth and expansion onto a national platform. The organization was prepared at all levels and was able to leverage the change rather than become paralyzed by it.

When processes are in place to regularly assess and improve the organization's response to change, thriving leadership practices become the standard at all levels. Consistent involvement in strategic planning and performance management activities assures that the Board and the current leader are moving the organization in the direction of a mission, vision and services that are still relevant in meeting the needs of stakeholders.

Start With the End in Mind

A young woman took the helm of a 25-year-old organization that had suffered tremendously after the disruptive departure of a long-standing leader. Following that transition, the organization had been through four different chief executives in five years.

From the outset, the new leader developed a vision about where she would want the organization to be 10 years down the road. The questions she raised made her board slightly nervous, given that they had experienced such significant turnover in chief executives. "I'm not going anywhere," she assured them, "but I do want to solidify the organization's legacy."

Collaborating with her board, the new leader worked backwards from her vision. Through a continual process and with much discussion, she figured out how to make changes in the organization's real estate holdings and consulted with the well-known head of a real estate firm to sell the existing facility and lease a new space.

She started a specific program to recruit strong talent and to manage that talent effectively with an eye toward leadership development. Every day, she kept both her strategic and leadership legacy plan in mind. And, she continued to strengthen the organization to achieve its current and long-term goals. Her legacy and the legacy of the organization were in complete alignment. When she left five years later, the organization was thriving.

The best interest of any organization is served both by starting where you are, and as Stephen Covey said, starting "with the end in mind."[2] What is the legacy that the organization wants to leave? What is the legacy that the leader wants to leave? How are they aligned? Are they achievable?

Readiness to take on change demands that the organization knows where they are and where they want to go. It also requires that they strive to build a foundation of organizational and fiscal effectiveness which supports progress. It's simple to understand, but hard to deliver. There are a lot of actions that go into implementation. There are many steps to take and just as many barriers and bumps to avoid, especially when the focus is on leadership change.

Illumination: Savvy chief executives spend time building relationships with their board members, sharing responsibility for guiding the organization. In the context of these partnerships, issues of legacy and transition become a natural part of the strategic discussion.

---

2 Covey, Stephen R. *Seven Habits of Highly Effective People*. Free Press, 1989.

— Chapter 2 —
Align the Legacies

The organization was created with a particular mission and vision for its work. For the founder or long-term leader, that mission and vision virtually flow through her DNA. Founders who start nonprofits from the ground up have a passion to serve others, to advocate for a cause, or to create economic empowerment, to name a few. They work tirelessly on behalf of the organization, particularly when it is in the start-up phase.

Their efforts are a labor of love, and many leaders talk about the satisfaction they derive from their roles. The boards of these organizations often include friends, colleagues and supporters of the chief executive who are connected through a personal relationship.

During these early stages in the organization's lifecycle, the founder is frequently the subject matter expert. The board often defers to the leader's desires when it comes to decision-making and strategic planning because of that expertise and because of the loyalty that flows from the personal relationship.

Over the years as the organization grows and more staff is added, the need for a clearer structure develops, requiring very different skills than those at start-up. The founder/leader is called upon to step-up his or her leadership competency, while the board needs to increase its ability to provide more objectivity with governance and oversight.

Monopolizing the Spotlight

This founder-led organization, based in Washington, DC, provides advocacy and programming globally to address sexual exploitation of women in developing nations. The founder, who was in her role for 25 years, talked a good game about sharing leadership responsibilities, but never really walked the talk.

Leadership development was at a minimum. In fact, while the founder spoke about cascading responsibility to the vice presidents to decrease her own role in operations, programming and fundraising, the opposite happened. As each of the vice presidents began to exert their leadership, the founder limited their responsibilities and challenged their authority. One by one, each vice president left.

The board was alerted to the issue of leadership depletion, but since they were dispersed globally, they were reluctant to address the organizational challenges. The founder was always the key spokesperson and major fundraiser, and no board members felt empowered to upset that scenario.

As funders began to question the impact and efficacy of the organization, the funding declined and the organization faced a crisis of sustainability. Once this reached epidemic proportions, the board addressed the impending crisis by asking the founder to step down. Sadly, the founder lost her stature as a compelling spokesperson and advocate. The destabilized organization hired new leadership but has yet to regain its revered place in the highly competitive global service sector. The accomplished and departed vice presidents became leaders in other national and global organizations that address women's sexual rights.

At the outset, the founder or long-term leader's legacy was tied to achieving the vision and mission. At this juncture, it becomes important for the board and the leader to realistically stop and assess what is in the best interest of the organization as it evolves. It is most critical that through these ongoing and realistic assessments, every organization develops the tools and strategies it needs to succeed beyond its founder or long-term leader.

Founder's Syndrome can also apply to a long-term leader, who took over from a founder and became responsible for navigating the organization's growth. The noteworthy symptom is that the organization continues to operate aligned with the unique personality of the chief executive (or long-term founding board). Decisions are often less visionary and instead often reflect a bootstrap mentality, desperately working to hold the organization together rather than taking the risks of moving forward. Most frequently, Founder's Syndrome occurs in organizations that have grown from a grassroots operation to approximately a $10 million community powerhouse.

Founder Without a Legacy

After almost 30 years, the founder of a $50M national nonprofit organization that coordinates neighborhood revitalization projects decided to step down. The organization was simply not prepared for the change. Although all members of the senior leadership team had been there for 10 to 20 years, no one had become a "number two." To complicate the matter, the board and executive committee had all been personally selected by and were emotionally connected to the founder/leader.

When the founder decided to leave, the board, and indirectly, the founder, enabled a worst-case scenario. An internal board search committee was formed. Even though the founder insisted she would not be involved in the search, she used her relationship with stakeholders to exert subtle influence on the selection process, which excluded staff input or representation. In fact, she had personally decided on a successor and strongly recommended that candidate to the search committee. The organization had no guidance from a search professional and had very minimal external stakeholder input. It was a typical case of *"Founder's Syndrome,"* where a

Founder Without a Legacy *continued*

long-term leader seeks to maintain disproportionate power and influence over the organization to the extent that he or she actually puts the organization in jeopardy.

The crisis set in for this board when they chose an external candidate without the blessing or approval of the exiting founder/leader. She then attempted to block the hire by continuing to advocate strongly for her recommended candidate.

With diverse opinions about the future direction of the organization, the board and the outgoing leader found themselves in a nasty end game. Although efforts were made to engage the founder/leader in the transition, she refused to participate in events and celebrations planned to honor her tenure and to welcome the new leader. She also demonstrated such a disregard for the wellbeing of the organization that she openly disparaged the board's newly selected successor within regional and national professional networks.

Because there had been such a sense of urgency to quickly name a successor, the staff and board began to second-guess their own decisions, creating fear and panic throughout the organization. It was only then that a professional leadership legacy planning consultant was brought in and asked to:

- develop a transition strategy in collaboration with board leadership.
- assess the senior leadership team's strengths.
- provide coaching throughout the leadership change for the overall organization. as well as the integration of the new chief executive.

After the founder/leader departed, the crisis worsened when a multitude of financial and organizational issues were discovered and required immediate attention. The problems were overwhelming

Founder Without a Legacy *continued*

and included difficulties with facilities, finances, funding, and staff competencies. Because the board leadership succession was also not planned and the end of the current board chair's term coincided with the departure of the found/leader, the new chief executive and a newly selected board chair were forced to navigate very rocky waters together.

The board and senior staff were in chaos throughout the transition. The founder/leader had committed financial resources to a failed initiative and continued to denigrate the board and new leadership. As a result, the new chief executive spent most of the first year addressing financial and relationship crises. She had little time to manage the on-boarding process for herself and even less time to create a new compelling vision for the organization. After two years, the organization is finally on more stable footing, and a new board chair who did not have a prior relationship with the founder/leader is in place.

Do No Harm

Forty years ago, a founder responded to a family member's dramatic health ordeal by creating a Phoenix, Arizona, nonprofit which provided advocacy and funded research for a rare immune disorder. Most board members had been personally affected by the disorder. When they could no longer serve, their children succeeded them. The organization had flourished with the founder as the face of the organization as well as the major fundraiser; but it was clear to the board and the leader that it was time to begin to prepare for leadership succession.

Prior attempts at leadership succession had not been successful because the executives chosen had been board members. There was not enough separation between the founder and the board members to allow a new executive to have the freedom necessary to explore new directions for the organization.

The founder and the board worked closely together on a transition plan to prepare for a successor. To create a more robust process, they were engaged in a search process to identify an external professional with the competencies that would complement the founder. Concurrently, the board worked to improve their governance and reduce the organization's reliance on the founder.

Once a new chief executive was ultimately hired, the founder was asked to develop a defined role focused on cultivating individual and corporate donors. Onboarding for the new CEO continued throughout the first year and included coaching on how to develop a constructive partnership with the founder.

The founder now serves as an advisor to the board but does not hold a board seat. She feels acknowledged for her contributions and has been publicly honored for her work. She has also been inspired to write her memoir, which can only continue to benefit both her own legacy and that of the organization.

Storm Cloud: Sometimes a founder or long-term leader who has been in her organization more than one or two decades has kept the founding board in place. Often the board chair has flourished in a leadership role for the length of that tenure. Unfortunately, while the long tenure of the founding board brings stability, it can also result in stagnation and the "rubberstamping" of the leader's strategy and decisions.

The organization must start from a point of truly understanding - and a willingness to address - the potential challenges it may face during the transition of a founder or long-term leader. Without full recognition of the challenges, organizations can succumb to very difficult times.

In reality, this means consistently assessing the performance of a founder or long-term leader to ensure that they are effectively driving the organization's growth and success. In many cases, the board goes on auto-pilot, accepting the current situation as the norm, without understanding the potential problems that may occur when the leader's focus is not aligned with the organization's needs.

— Chapter 3 —
Helping the Leader Find His or Her Way

When a founder or long-term leader tries to maintain disproportionate power and influence over the organization, the dysfunction is palpable. Some of the main clues that this may be the case are:

- the organization has become exclusively identified with the founder/leader.
- it is reactive, rather than proactive.
- all critical decision-making is centralized with the founder/leader without real input from staff or board.
- the founder/leader is surrounded by cheerleaders at the board and staff level where loyalty (rather than good ideas and ongoing feedback) is the most important value.
- no succession plan exists.
- there is limited professional development for current staff leadership.
- the board often "rubber stamps" the founder/leader's actions and does not probe basic financial or programmatic questions.

Storm Cloud: A failure to realistically assess the alignment of the organization's and leader's legacies can create a crisis when the founder/leader decides to leave. The mad scramble to manage leadership change and address succession is accompanied by a sense of panic and urgency.

It is fairly common that a founder or long-term leader simply does not know how to gracefully give up the reins. Often, this is because his or her personal sense of self-worth is still tied to the organization. It is in the best interest of the organization to try and support the leader in seeing the positive benefits of a transition away from the organization and to recognize that the organization will also benefit from fresh thinking.

Robert M. Galford and Regina Fazio Maruca, authors of *Your Leadership Legacy*, argue that our leadership legacy is something that we should be thinking about right now. They say it's never too early to make a legacy plan and follow it – an approach they call "legacy thinking."[3] This planning involves taking the long view of the organization and asking what the lasting impact could be on the organization and the people. This legacy thinking can influence daily behaviors. Jim Kouzes and Barry Posner, authors of *A Leader's Legacy*, indicate that legacies are not the result of wishful thinking, but the result of "wishful doing." They state, "the legacy you leave is the life you lead."[4]

Illumination: When board leaders understand and practice sound nonprofit board governance, they have robust conversations with the chief executive on a regular basis, and not just during the performance review. These conversations include discussions about the organization's legacy, its current life stage, and what it will need to thrive. This can also open the door to talking about tougher issues, including the future plans of the founder or long-term leader.

Thinking about how to move on while leaving a legacy can be a source of anxiety for long-term leaders. Executives who do make a successful transition at the end of their run often focus from the very beginning of their tenure on the kind of legacy they want to leave behind. They set their sights on the finish line early on. It is a powerful experience for these leaders to engage with their peers in roundtable formats where they can benefit from shared wisdom and have the opportunity to be honest, reflective and vulnerable, knowing that others will challenge their thinking in a supportive environment. These interactions with peers are often better than trying to process the legacy/succession/retirement

---

3 Galford, Robert M. and Maruca, Regina Fazio. Your Leadership Legacy. Harvard Business School, 2006.

4 Kouzes, Jim and Posner, Barry. A Leader's Legacy. Josey-Bass, 2006.

thinking internally with staff or board members who may feel anxious about the conversation, or may not feel at liberty to provide honest and objective feedback.

In a series of focus groups with founders and long-term leaders[5], the majority articulated that they indeed felt that their personal legacy was tied to achieving the mission of their organizations. Looking into the future, some believed that the organization could achieve its mission without requiring them to stay at the helm; others were not so sure. The truth is that if an organization cannot thrive without its original founder or long-term leader, that founder has done a grave disservice to the very organization that has been at the heart of her passion and dedication.

But what happens when the organization's mission diverges from the founder or long-term leader's goals? What happens when the leader's personal mission is no longer aligned with the organization's mission? Or even when a founder or long-term leader's very skill set is no longer in sync with the reality of the organization's current needs?

For founders and long-term leaders who are thinking about moving on, there is no question that raising the issue of the alignment of personal and organizational legacy can be a source of anxiety. But it doesn't have to be. Asking the questions and having the discussion only strengthens the sustainable longevity of the organization. It is important to figure out what is best for the organization without confusing those interests with the founder/long-term leader's personal legacy or ego needs. The only real way to do that is if we understand what is driving the leader.

Whether he recognizes it or not, a founder or long-term leader is creating a legacy. When he leaves the organization, people will have a strong opinion of his contribution. Proactively, there are some questions that can initiate the discussion about that contribution:

- Is the legacy of the founder/leader a personal legacy, an organizational legacy, or both?

---

5 Rosenwald and Mallow Wendell conducted focus groups in 2005 and 2006.

- How can these legacies be mutually inclusive?
- How are they currently mutually *exclusive*?
- What kind of organization does the founder/leader want to leave behind?
- For what does he want to be remembered?
- What is the impact she wanted achieve? For her own personal sense of accomplishment and for others?

Storm Cloud: Some leaders may use the organization as a launching pad for the building of a personal presence, regionally or nationally – rather than investing time and effort to support the real mission.

The challenge occurs when the leader focuses on his personal legacy at the expense of the organization, or simply avoids considering how the organization will flourish once he leaves.

When executives connect their leadership to personal *and* organizational legacy, their nonprofits are positioned to flourish. When a board encourages the alignment and the integration of these perspectives, it can also re-energize a long-term leader and reinvigorate staff.

While the divergence in the personal and organizational legacy may not be as obvious during the years of the founder/leader's reign, it can become incredibly challenging during a time of leadership transition. Current research, including the Annie E. Casey Foundation's work[6], clearly demonstrates that a transition in leadership occurs more effectively and effortlessly when the leader's legacy is aligned and integrated with that of the organization.

When executives see their leadership as integral to crafting their legacy, they become free to respond to opportunities and move in new

---

6 Adams, Tom. "Founder Transitions: Creating Good Endings and New Beginnings." The Annie E. Casey Foundation, Evelyn and Walter Haas, Jr. Fund, Executive Transitions Monograph Series, 2005.

directions. There is nothing more important for a leader than to position the organization to flourish well beyond her tenure. To do that means leaders need to own the vision, develop the organization's talent, and assist the board in driving leadership legacy and succession planning. It also means that the leader has to seriously think about how the organization will thrive beyond her tenure and know that this thinking and planning is an essential part of her own personal legacy.

It is important for the personal goals of the chief executive to be aligned with the organization's short- and long-term needs. The following discussion points can stimulate the thinking of the leader and the board chair at the outset of the legacy planning process:

- **What aspects of the current leadership role provide the greatest satisfaction for the chief executive?** What does the leader find the most enjoyable? What are the competencies and talents that he or she brings? What is the best way to harness the leader's energy and creativity? What blocks him or her from making the best contribution?
- **What does the organization need the most to thrive?** Are the organization's resources aligned with the strategic planning goals? Does the organization's structure and operating systems ensure effective service and program delivery? Where are the gaps?
- **How is the organization perceived by the immediate and larger community?** Are the mission and messaging clear? How do the programs deliver positively on the desired outcomes? Do board and staff share a consistent message with stakeholders and extended constituents?
- **How does the leadership want to be viewed by external partners and stakeholders?** Is regular feedback solicited/ received from a diverse group of direct reports, colleagues and board members? What leadership aspects need to be strengthened? What developmental opportunities should be considered?

Moving forward, outline the concrete steps that will strengthen the organization and the chief executive's alignment of personal and professional goals. If that is not possible, focus on strengthening the organization in a way that will create a smooth transition.

- **Create a roundtable of trusted advisors.** No one can be successful alone. Establish or find a trusted group of individuals with whom to share personal and organizational concerns. Consider a mentor or thought partner. Think about the colleagues who can provide inspiration, challenge current thinking, and offer strategic approaches to professional challenges. This roundtable can be a regularly scheduled group or individuals who provide constructive feedback on a consulting basis.
- **Create the right organizational structure to achieve optimal results.** It is critical for the organization's infrastructure to reflect what is required to achieve the established mission. Are there clearly defined roles and responsibilities for staff at all levels that emanate from organizational goals? Does leadership cascade down through the senior team? Is there transparency around goals and processes? What opportunities do staff have for input and decision-making into their responsibilities and approaches within the context of organizational goals?
- **Promote better transparency, accountability and decision-making throughout the organization**. What is the best way to convey tangible and cultural information throughout all levels of the staff? Does the staff know how decisions are made? How could more timely and accurate information impact productivity, collaboration and commitment?
- **Cultivate talent.** Prior to a founder's exit, successive leadership can be developed. The current leader can identify and assess potential leaders, evaluate who is the strongest, develop a growth path through delegation and coaching, and strengthen board skills. If part of the founder/leader's personal legacy is to create a well-managed, well-led organization, this approach will be a natural part of talent cultivation.
- **Create the next series of strategic steps.** The organization must keep moving forward or it will not continue to thrive. Build the organization's strength so that it is prepared for innovation and reasonable risk. Engage in frequent discussions about strategy, and

review and update the formal strategic plan on a regular basis.

- **Engage the board in helping to identify strategic opportunities.** Ask the hard questions. Is the mission still relevant? Are the programs and services aligned with the mission, or is there evidence of mission creep brewing within?
- **Evaluate the external environment.** Are there new developments in regulations or funding that might impact the organization? What is the competitive landscape - are similar organizations providing comparable services aimed at the same audience? How is the organization positioned in the larger community? Is the organization appropriately networked within the sector as well as in the broader community at the local, state and national levels?
- **Identify potential new opportunities.** Consider new partnerships and expanded collaborative possibilities with other nonprofit and for profit organizations, funders and individuals to reduce expenses or increase revenue. How can you successfully leverage the board and senior team in this process?
- **Assess the organization's risk tolerance.** An independent consultant can conduct an assessment as part of a strategic planning or organizational review to determine resiliency and preparation for managing risks associated with change.

Consciously creating a legacy plan and connecting that to the success and sustainability of the organization will pave the way for a smooth transition when the executive director decides to move on. It is essential to have an action plan in place that incorporates both personal and organizational legacies. Make sure that the plan includes ongoing, regularly scheduled time to reflect on movement towards the goals and preparation for the future.

Devoting time for the deliberate review of where the executive director is and where she is going organizationally and personally will free her up to know that even when she is no longer at the helm, she will be leaving the organization in good shape to achieve its goals and mission.

— Chapter 4 —
Plan for Succession. Plan for Success.

Most organizations behave as though the right time to address a leadership change is when a leader announces he is planning to depart. Unfortunately, starting that late in the game can easily thrust the organization into a state of flux, which will negatively impact staff, stakeholders and the ability to function effectively through the transition period. It doesn't make sense.

Storm Cloud:
While organizations would never dream of eliminating their insurance policies, many don't have a succession plan to manage temporary or permanent leadership contingencies, although a change in leadership is just as critical to long-term sustainability.

Typically, an organization will have two types of succession plans. One is an *emergency succession plan*, designed to provide a roadmap for the organization to continue operations in the event of an unplanned absence or sudden departure of the chief executive or a key manager. The second is the *comprehensive succession plan*, which focuses on the permanent departure of the chief executive and involves a process for cultivating and developing leadership talent within the organization. The comprehensive succession plan creates the potential for an internal successor while leaving the door open to search externally for a replacement.

The emergency succession plan differs from the comprehensive succession plan by specifically noting the steps required to ensure that the organization continues to operate smoothly after an unexpected change in leadership for at least six weeks to four months. By thinking through how to continue in an emergency, the organization gains valuable insight into its longer-term succession plan. Questions to inform the creation of the succession plans appear in Appendix (B).

To Identify or Not to Identify a Successor

There is much debate in the corporate and nonprofit worlds regarding the best way to select and groom a successor.

In corporate boardrooms, organizations evaluate skills, experience, and values based on a "success profile," to ensure that the right candidates are groomed for succession as CEO. Boards look two to three years ahead to identify a baseline of key behaviors for evaluating potential candidates. In this way, they retain executives who are part of an effective succession planning process. In fact, investors have demonstrated that they will penalize companies without a defined succession plan.

There is always the question about whether or not the optimal successor will be an internal or an external candidate. Sometimes the actual "heir apparent," who is being groomed by the founder or long-term leader, may not have the leadership competencies required for success in the top role. Or sometimes the senior leaders are there more as a result of inertia or loyalty, and are no longer making a meaningful and productive contribution to the organization.

Good succession planning means that organizations identify future leaders and ensure their continued growth and development. In this way, potential leaders can prepare to successfully take the helm, either on a temporary basis to fill an unplanned leave of absence, or to permanently replace an outgoing chief executive. Successful nonprofits offer ongoing opportunities for growth, advancement and financial rewards to keep potential successors invested for the long-term.

In many smaller organizations, succession planning may be viewed as a luxury, but it isn't. It's essential. At the very least, the board of directors has a responsibility to consider and plan for the departure of the executive director. In some instances, the board may decide that there needs to be a "second in command" who has the capacity to step into the lead in the future. This means:

- identifying that person in collaboration with the executive director.
- confirming that the person is motivated to take on the top job.
- developing a plan to ensure that the eventual successor will gain the requisite skills and knowledge to assume the role.
- exposing him or her to a broad range of different experiences to fully comprehend the operations of the organization.

The plan for developing a second in command could include a formalized process of mentoring/coaching and training in the nuances of moving into the chief executive role. When the size of the organization permits, it is preferable to have more than one person identified as a potential successor. In a small nonprofit, it may not be possible to groom an internal successor. If that is the case, multiple senior team members can be cross-trained to assure the breadth of the organization's operation is covered, thereby ensuring continuity and stability.

It is critical to an organization's sustainability to think about succession as a fact of life. An effective succession plan focuses on how to best help the organization continue to thrive and achieve its mission. More than a singular act of how to replace the current leader, the succession plan is a dedicated process to map the landscape, prepare for contingencies, and minimize potentially negative issues that can affect the organization.

Succession planning should always be a part of the strategic planning conversation. It is not easy work and does require receptivity and candid conversations between the leader and the board chair to address the reality of the situation. It also demands a willingness, dedication and discipline on the part of the board and the chief executive to build a solid foundation together for the good of the organization by setting realistic goals and developing leadership potential at all levels of the organization. An organization that addresses succession issues honestly and transparently, before a founder or long-term leader departs, will position itself positively for change. The following questions represent a starting point to discuss where the organization is with regard to actively planning for succession. Please indicate a response to the organization's current status using the scale below.

Succession Planning

1 = Never 2 = Infrequently 3 = Not Sure
4 = Frequently 5 = Consistently

a.　The organization has included succession planning in the strategic or other planning processes. _____

b.　The board of directors initiates discussions about leadership legacy planning with the chief executive. _____

c.　The chief executive initiates leadership legacy planning discusions with the board. _____

d.　Legacy leadership discussions include staff beyond the chief executive. _____

e.　Senior staff is engaged and visible to external partnerships and constituencies. _____

f.　The organization evaluates and manages employee performance. _____

g.　The organization identifies potential talent and develops staff at the senior and middle levels. _____

h.　Senior staff members in the organization have access to opportunities to develop their leadership potential (i.e. coaching, education, experiences). _____

i.　Team leaders are held accountable for coaching and developing their direct reports. _____

j.　The board reviews and updates its governance plan (including term limits). _____

Succession Planning *continued*

1 = Never 2 = Infrequently 3 = Not Sure
4 = Frequently 5 = Consistently

k. The board evaluates its process to manage its own   _____
    leadership succession.

l. The board engages in self-assessment of its performance.   _____

m. The board engages in yearly assessment of its   _____
    executive director.

n. The board of directors has a strategy in place for   _____
    recruiting, orienting and developing new board members.

Total Score   _____

Scoring

A score of 65 – 70 The organization is in excellent condition to
manage succession.

A score of 50 – 64 Assess the lower scores to determine where to
focus succession planning efforts.

A score of 40 – 49 The organization may be at risk of struggling
through a potential transition. Determine where
it needs to start to create a viable plan
for succession.

39 points or less The organization could be at serious risk. Review
the chapter on how to create a succession plan to
identify key activities to improve the situation.

Surprise! The Balance Sheet Isn't as Good as You Thought

A passionate business leader based in New York City founded a charitable organization focused on memoir and the arts. When the governance structure for the organization was created, legal counsel advised the founder to assume the joint roles of Executive Director and Board Chair to secure his leadership. This model was ineffective because the founder was stretched thin, managing both the administration of the staff and overseeing governance.

As the organization began to seek funding from foundations, concerns about the dual roles surfaced. Over time, the board structure evolved. A Board Chair was elected to oversee governance and support the founder. The founder, however, was resistant to the new structure. He was reluctant to share relevant information and engage the board regarding the status of finances and operations. He believed that the board's only role was fundraising. As typical of many organizations with founder-selected boards, many of the board members who had been recruited by the founder were reluctant to challenge him.

After leading the organization for almost a decade, the founder suffered a health crisis that limited his involvement in the operations. When the board became more engaged in the administration to provide support in his absence, they discovered that major financial planning had been ignored. The founder subsequently gave notice and the board began the process of managing a leadership transition. At the very same time, they became aware that the organization was carrying a significant financial deficit. Suddenly they were faced with the challenge of attempting to bring in top prospective candidates while confronting a dire financial reality. In addition, the board had to deal with the founder's expectation that they would choose an internal candidate he had groomed and recommended, and that the founder himself would continue with the organization as a paid consultant.

Surprise! The Balance Sheet Isn't as Good as You Thought *continued*

The board stepped up to the challenges. They simultaneously addressed the recruitment needs and the financial management issues. A new executive director was hired following a robust external search. She had full knowledge of the challenges and opportunities. A compromise was reached with the outgoing founder regarding a limited consulting contract for a specific project.

The deficit was addressed by creating a special fund to honor the vision of the founder. In just one year, the new executive director was successfully leading the organization and staff in new directions and had forged a strong partnership with the board.

Storm Cloud: Rather than seizing the opportunity for review and reflection by engaging an interim director, boards too often move forward and rush to fill the leadership vacuum out of a deep sense of panic.

If succession planning is inadequate or non-existent, it can create a mad scramble when the founder or long-term leader decides to leave the organization. Too often, a sense of deep panic sets in because the staff and board are unsure how to run the organization without its current leader. This doesn't have to be the case. Strong leadership among the staff and the board can ensure the organization's stability and ongoing sustainability. Ideally, if faced with this difficult situation, the board will create an interim leadership plan to give the organization the breathing time it needs to focus on its future.

Storm Cloud: Interim executive directors are trained professionals with a defined skill set and experience; they are not simply board members or internal staff who assume the place of the chief executive until the permanent successor is identified.

A change in leadership offers an opportunity that rarely comes along. It allows the board the time to check in, re-evaluate, reaffirm the mission, and review both the strategic and tactical paths forward.

Interim directors provide a different and, often, very helpful way to calm the panic and allow the organization the breathing room it needs. Skilled managers and former chief executives are available for these roles, and can temporarily (six to nine months) help the board and staff address critical operational, organizational and human resource issues, and lay the groundwork for the permanent leader's success.

A competent external interim can facilitate changes that can help turn around an organization in crisis. In stable organizations, the interim can provide an important respite between a founder, or other "big shoes" leader, and his/her successor.

An Identified Internal Candidate

You have identified an internal candidate, or a member of the senior management team or the board has stepped forward. Why invest in an executive search?

Organizations may believe that retaining an executive search firm is unnecessary if an internal candidate has surfaced. To the contrary, conducting a wider search and engaging a search consultant to manage it can be particularly useful to assure a comprehensive, consistent process. It is important to manage expectations fully and transparent-ly for both the internal and external stakeholders. Internal candidates should know that the search process will be the same for them as for

Storm Cloud: If the internal candidate is not handled properly, the outcome is major fall-out and resistance among the staff, affecting the ability of the new CEO to lead.

external candidates. Using an outside search consultant helps to guarantee this. It also makes it easier for the board to have a "neutral" party managing the process.

A search process is particularly useful if the outgoing CEO has selected an individual to become his or her successor. In most cases, this evokes concern among staff, board members or stakeholders that the "hand-picked" CEO will lead in ways identical to the exiting long-term/founder CEO. When the internal candidate is vetted through a uniform, comprehensive interviewing process, it gives them the opportunity to describe their own vision and the ways that they would approach leadership differently from their predecessor. A search consultant is better able to tease out the critical leadership competencies than a board member.

When an external candidate prevails in the search process, the consultant can handle the communication with the internal staff member in effective ways that result in positive outcomes, and the ability for the internal candidate to work harmoniously with the new chief executive.

In the event that the internal applicant emerges as the selected candidate, all constituencies can be confident that he or she was vetted and found to be entirely qualified and ready to take on the leadership role. With either outcome, the new CEO emerging from a full search has a much better foundation to start in the role, and generally receives greater support from stakeholders.

Cautionary Tale: Board Member Serving as Interim

A museum/theater in New York City had a beloved chief executive. The organization had been dependent on her for over 20 years with no attention paid to succession planning. When the chief executive suddenly died, a long-time, well-heeled member of the board stepped up to assume the interim leadership role. This board member had been a major donor to the organization and commanded a large circle of supportive fundraising friends. During the search process, the acting interim decided to throw his hat into the ring as the permanent replacement. He was given consideration for the role of chief executive, but in the end was not selected as the best choice for the position.

The interim executive immediately resigned from the board taking his large circle of fundraising friends with him. This became a big challenge for the new chief executive and the board. The effectiveness of the board and its fundraising efforts were greatly diminished, taking more than five years to get back on track.

Cultivate Talent

A vibrant organization has strong, strategic leaders who recognize the importance of continual talent cultivation. They foster a culture of growth and development for all managers and staff which cascades leadership development to all levels. This includes creating an environment where each staff member experiences a sense of ownership, leadership, responsibility and accountability and is supported in knowing that he or she is a valued contributing member of the team.

The opportunity for individuals at all levels to exercise leadership brings out the best strengths of those involved and reduces the sense of frustration that can occur when information and decision-making are concentrated in the hands of the founder or long-term leader. Effective leaders know the importance of sharing information and decision-making with their boards and staffs. This is especially true when more dramatic changes occur in the organization. It is a much better experience for each individual to be on board and to contribute positively to the evolution of the organization than to feel forced into a corner by changes other people have initiated with little input into the future. Often, the impetus to identify potential leaders and address their professional development comes from the recognition that a change in leadership might take place.

Leadership development doesn't just happen. It takes a strategic view to understand how to bring in new talent and cultivate existing talent. Talent cultivation is an essential component to a thriving organization's culture. While effective talent development may be focused within the organization, the cultivation and development of talent on the board is equally important. The key to ensuring leadership cultivation is to create and maintain robust performance appraisal and management systems for the staff and the board.

Uniform and timely processes help to assess the effectiveness of leadership development. These should cascade from the board to the chief executive, and from the chief executive to senior leadership. Processes should be based on clearly defined goals, enabling the organization to realistically mark what is working and what needs to be refined. Goals, objectives and expectations must be articulated, and each person's performance should be evaluated against them.

The performance management system should both measure accomplishments and prescribe appropriate development opportunities, goals and objectives for every staff member, beginning with the chief executive. A robust board assessment can evaluate the collective work of the board and delineate how the board can increase its performance on behalf of the organization.

When regular evaluation and development of the growth of each staff member is in place, the chief executive can be at liberty to look more broadly at how he or she can create an organizational culture focused on the continued building and expansion of that talent. The bottom line is that every organization should have a process and plan in place to invest in their staff.

- Does the organization embrace a learning culture, continually looking for opportunities that enable staff to cultivate strengths?
- Are staff given opportunities to grow and learn new skills?
- Do development opportunities include involvement in decision-making and shared leadership, such as rotating facilitation of staff meetings?
- How can staff roles in decision-making be expanded?
- Are senior staff members specifically evaluated on their ability to provide coaching and development for their direct reports?
- Does the organization support staff in volunteering outside the organization, such as participating on other boards or committees to broaden their perspective and skills?
- Does the organization have a proscribed process to identify and develop individuals who demonstrate greater than average potential talent by creating stretch goals and growth opportunities?
- Does the board manage its own talent effectively? Is there a process in place for orienting new board members and engaging them in growth opportunities?
- Does the board assess its own performance on a regular basis?

The best way to support talent cultivation and align individual and organizational growth is by establishing thriving leadership practices. When organizations invest in the growth and development of staff, they stand a better chance of attracting and retaining talent. The practices do involve a consistency in commitment and an investment of time, but they do not have to be financially burdensome; there are many creative ways to procure these services. The process of investing in staff development includes the ability to:

- **Identify, assess and develop new leaders.** The organization should evaluate and decide what type of coaching, training and other opportunities are available to build capacity at all levels in the organization. Capacity-building grants, funders and other organizations can provide cost-effective opportunities for talent development. Additionally the organization's board members may be able to include one or two staff members in trainings or educational opportunities offered at their own workplace.

- **Evaluate the strongest performers.** By developing a performance management system, the organization can provide opportunities that support those with the strongest potential to move forward by participating in activities to achieve leadership goals. Feedback from direct reports, peers/colleagues and supervisors will provide the broadest perspective of who should be on the list and how they are performing on an ongoing basis.
- **Establish clear performance goals for every staff member.** This can include quarterly and mid-year goal setting to personally challenge each individual to achieve new skills and competencies and assume responsibilities that reinforce his or her growth and development.
- **Evaluate goals yearly.** This will provide concrete data to measure the successes and necessary refinements for the board and chief executive.
- **Create ongoing leadership opportunities.** Delegate and cross-train staff with the assignment of new projects or initiatives, training or education, and service, (which can even be placements on boards or committees outside of the organization). When an organization determines the strategic and tactical tasks that should be handled by members of the senior management team, leadership opportunities can be identified, and staff can receive the development support they need to get ready to assume those responsibilities.
- **Regular assessment of the board and its members.** Benchmark the board's existing talent and level of participation, and evaluate which skills, competencies and demographics are still missing. Cultivate desirable new board recruits. Once identified, create a plan to reach out and engage them, first on committees and then onto the board.
- **Strengthen board skills.** Create a successful board orientation and integration process, as well as a board succession plan. Support board members in developing their knowledge of and competency in sound governance. Encourage every board member to be involved in strategic planning and to understand the financial status of the organization.

- **Develop a systematic approach to coaching and feedback.** This should occur throughout the organization, cascading to all levels from the board to the chief executive, from the chief executive to senior management.

When talent management is integrated into all aspects of the organization, at the staff and board levels, the organization will thrive and position itself to handle change with agility and resilience. Good talent management processes ease the issues around succession for the chief executive, as well as other senior leaders in the organization, and ensures that the relationship between the board and the professional staff becomes both supportive and appropriately challenging.

Build a Great Board

As organizations position for leadership change, the board's role can sometimes be overlooked. A vibrant, engaged board can help an organization approach a transition and support the positive process of creating a leadership legacy.

It is equally important that the board have a specific development plan to manage and cultivate its own talent. Does the board identify potential members and manage its own talent effectively? Is there a consistent process in place for orienting new board members? Does the board assess its *own* performance on a regular basis?

It is essential that the goals and vision for the organization are shared between the board and staff and that the energy and effort expended focus on achieving positive results. Some of the ways to utilize the best resources of each group and to create a strong, shared partnership are to:

- clearly define expectations between the chief executive and key board leadership.
- create alignment between the organization's mission, its drive to be sustainable, and the talent and resources needed.
- establish collaborative annual performance expectations for the founder/leader and assess his or her performance using a process that gains input from staff and key stakeholders.

- establish collaborative annual goals and expectations for the board and assess its performance against those, ideally using a process to gain input from staff and key stakeholders.
- internally and/or through external consultation, offer the necessary strategic support and coaching to the founder/leader and to the board chair to optimize their performances.

It is valuable to determine how to support the growth and development of the board as a significant and positive contributor to the organization. Encouraging the training and effective participation of members creates a board that will contribute significantly to the governance of the organization.

The long-term leader or founder may actually not be receptive to board oversight because he has been steering the ship without involving the board in critical strategic, financial or capacity decisions. Many board chairs of high profile organizations who have long-term relationships with the leader do fall in line with that same thinking, avoiding the responsibility of serious oversight. *The Perfect Storm—or How to Plan a Leadership Crisis*[7] describes how many boards ignore the discussion of succession planning for fear of rocking the boat with the current leadership.

When boards skip succession planning and steer into *the perfect storm*, they guarantee a rocky ride filled with surprises for stakeholders on the horizon. While leadership legacy planning may not be one of the top priorities of many boards, it is one of the basics that needs to be discussed and put in place to avoid this trap.

Without a steady hand at the helm, the organization's internal resources will be sapped by a leadership change, thrusting it into limbo with a high level of uncertainty. The cumulative cost is high staff and board turnover, lost revenue, and missed opportunities for program development and growth.

---

7 Rosenwald, Priscilla and Wendell, Lesley Mallow, "The Perfect Storm," TransitionWorks newsletter, 2007.

For some organizations, the chaos and ensuing crisis management actually serve as an adrenalin rush, distracting the board from its primary responsibilities of navigating the ship and charting the organization's future course. A basic primer for board governance and for the board members' individual responsibility is to:

- **Know the bylaws.** Bylaws can provide a roadmap to work through difficult situations. All board members should be clear about their responsibilities and expectations prior to installation. The bylaws should specify the code of ethics and how the board will assess its own performance. They should also outline the specific expected duties and functions of the board of directors as a whole to provide the continuity of mission for the organization.
- **Use the bylaws effectively.** The organization's bylaws should provide structural requirements, including the number of board members and sources of directors (i.e. community representatives) and defined board term limits, which provide both an opportunity to regularly reinvigorate the board, as well as to transition off ineffective members. The bylaws should also stipulate how often the board and its committees should meet.

Illumination: Successful boards hold annual retreats. These are not just extended board meetings, but real opportunities to engage in conversations about how to work together as an effective team, in collaboration with senior leadership. They are also the occasion to take a strategic view of participation, responsibility and accountability for the upcoming time period, along with goals and strategies.

- **Distinguish between governance and operations.** The executive director is the liaison between the board and the staff and has oversight of daily operational activities. The board's role is limited to governance. This includes how to select and appoint the executive director, govern the organization, and acquire sufficient resources, including financing of operations and accounting for expenditures.

- **Adopt a system for conducting meetings.** Structure debate, the decision-making process and board protocol by ensuring that board members adeptly use *Robert's Rules of Order*. This structure has rescued many meetings from chaos.

As the organization's governance needs evolve, the board should wean itself from involvement in operations and into more strategic governance. Board governance is the antidote to avoid the rocky waters and uncertain terrain. It is the essential frontline to support the organization's wellbeing. Board leadership requires strategic thinking, capable navigation, and the ability to take the helm in stormy seas or sometimes, even more importantly, to use its skills and thoughtful planning to avoid them.

Imagine a board shocked when the organization hits stormy weather or the leader exits dramatically. What a surprise if these boards subsequently discover financial mismanagement and any of the ravages of autocratic leadership, including poor morale and ailing programs/services. At that point, the board, which is ultimately responsible for the welfare of the organization, calls for "all hands on deck" and frantically seeks a turn-around skipper. Strong strategic governance can strengthen the organization's viability and create solid preparation to avoid this kind of frantic situation.

Succession planning should not just be a plan for an executive leadership transition at the staff level; it should also include the board. Thriving leadership practices recommend creating a board succession plan that involves an inventory of the current directors' skills and attributes as they match up with the organization's needs. This inventory will outline: the professional skills that make up a high-performing board (accounting, legal, HR, marketing, etc.); the talents that directors will be required to use (e.g. networking, connections, strategic thinking); and the demographic characteristics that each director represents (male/female, age, race, ethnicity, geographic location, etc.).

A high-performing, conscientious board will develop a succession plan to identify sources for potential board members who fulfill those key requirements. This succession plan enables the board to continue its work on behalf of the organization without disruption, meeting the business challenges they encounter.

The succession plan determines how to select and appoint new directors in an efficient and structured manner. Additionally, the plan will provide parameters for their ongoing appointment, an evaluation of how to assess which current board members have clear leadership expectations, and the ways to promote new potential leaders to make effective contributions.

The key questions when developing a succession plan for directors include:

- What are the skills, talents and attributes that the organization requires?
- Where are the people with these skills, talents and attributes?
- Once the right people have been identified, how can they be attracted to the board?
- How can new board members be integrated in a way that engages them and gives them the skills and knowledge to effectively govern?

The best way to move the responsibility for succession planning forward is to create a specific board committee, often called the nomination, succession planning or governance committee, that:

- develops a continuous list of eligible board candidates.
- interviews potential candidates.
- checks each candidate's references and board accomplishments.
- recommends candidates to the full board.
- ensures each new board member receives a comprehensive orientation.
- arranges ongoing board training and development activities.

Storm Cloud: Individuals elected to leadership positions who are risk-averse or adversarial might cause the organization to miss strategic and advantageous opportunities. In executive board roles, individuals who do not have effective leadership may create organizational dysfunction that can take years to reverse, if ever.

The governance or nominating committee is responsible for board recruitment and the annual/bi-annual performance reviews of board members. The committee should recommend any alterations to the functions and responsibilities of the board of directors as the organization grows beyond its start-up founder.

A nominating committee should also continuously assess current board members' performance, as delineated by defined expectations, i.e. attendance at board and committees meetings, participation at organization events, fundraising goals, and the participation and contribution he or she makes as a team member.

There is an increasing demand for highly qualified, dedicated, conscientious and aware directors who can add value to an organization. Failure to attract these people to the board can result in a lack of sustainability planning, disaffected funders, disengaged staff, and even the demise of the charitable organization.

Board members who do possess the desired interpersonal skills, intellectual abilities and other key attributes should be identified by the executive leadership long before they are asked to assume a higher leadership position. These individuals can be put at the front of the line as committee chairs and for other leadership opportunities. In some organizations, just like the staff leadership development, board members can also be informally assigned to a mentor, a current leader who will guide them in developing the additional skills they need.

Most organizations can survive a board member or two whose group participation skills and leadership attributes turn out to be less developed, by relying on the stronger members to neutralize any adverse consequences to the organization. However, placing brand new board members into the organization's highest leadership positions is a much riskier proposition. While this might work in rare instances, it does need to be carefully considered.

Selecting officers, most critically the board chair and vice chair, must be a thoughtful and strategic process. At times, being the chair or vice chair of a board demands exceptional and super-hero qualities, endless energy, undivided attention and a significant time commitment. These senior leadership positions are much more than high profile business opportunities. Accepting the responsibility of leading a nonprofit board, not just serving as a figurehead, assumes that the chair has demonstrated professional or volunteer leadership competencies - such as leading a team, running a business, and allocating resources to effectively produce results.

Illumination: When a board has an excellent reputation in the community for practicing good board governance, talented people are more drawn to serving on it for professional development and personal rewards.

Illumination: There are a number of board training opportunities that exist locally and nationally. Often, sponsored by foundations. Encourage your board members, especially new directors, to attend one of these "board boot camps."

The organization needs a safety-net process that gives these valued board leaders a chance to demonstrate their leadership skills in settings that do not put the organization at great risk, and where leadership failures will not cause irreparable harm.

Boards of successful organizations do not leave board leadership to chance. These organizations orient new board members, provide ongoing training to update governance capacity, and avoid leaving the selection of candidates for important leadership positions to the uncertainty of an open nominating process. Instead, they rely on a committee of knowledgeable and experienced board members to nominate a slate of candidates.

All of this is based on the understanding the critical importance of developing leaders, building a strategic partnership between staff and board, and creating an organization that will thrive, even if current leadership changes.

— Chapter 5 —
Kickstart Leadership Transition

As soon as it becomes known that the founder or long-term leader will be exiting the organization, active transition planning should begin. This planning is usually done by the leader in collaboration with the board, the board's transition planning committee, and/or with guidance from an external transition consultant.

Storm Cloud: Generally it is not positive for retiring founders and chief executives to stay on in an advisory capacity, either on the board or as a consultant. The continued presence of the former leader too often stymies the integration of the new leader.

To ensure leadership strength and continuity and to reduce the dependence on the long-term incumbent, the recommendation is for planning to begin 12 to 18 months prior to the leader's departure. The steps to achieve a smooth transition are to:

- Have the leader identify what can be realistically accomplished in the next 12 to 18 months toward established legacy goals.
- Review the current succession plan to determine the strength of the current senior leadership team. Determine if any of the other senior executives may be nearing retirement, contemplating a career move, or will be available to take on more leadership responsibilities.
- Create the transition plan. Do not leave it to the last minute or even to the last six months. While starting the search for a successor, determine whether the organization would benefit from an interim director.
- Outline the ongoing role of the retiring/exiting chief executive leading up to and following his or her departure.
- Determine the specifics of hiring a new executive. Will the organization choose an external search firm? Will a search committee be formed? Will the entire board be actively involved?

Even with a search firm, the board or its appointed search/transition committee should direct the process.
- Write a detailed communications plan for the staff and board as part of the transition plan. This plan should include message points that clearly reflect the concerns of those impacted. It should explain the reasons for the executive transition to key stakeholders and set the tone and vision for the organization with an introduction of the new team.
- Monitor the transition plan and update it regularly to reflect the evolving internal and external factors.

The desires and needs of the long-term leader and of the organization will direct the actions necessary to ensure a smooth transition. Both the outgoing leader and the transition team can use these key discussion points to start planning:

- Why is this the right time to transition leadership to a new chief executive?
- What would a successful leadership transition look like to the board and to the leader?
- What are the biggest challenges for a successful leadership transition?
- What can the leader do to support adequate succession planning? The board? The staff?
- How does the leader envision initiating the transition while still being embedded in the organization? Is this the optimal way for the organization to benefit?
- What will be the most difficult aspects for the leader in stepping back? How might this impact the organization?
- What will ensure the organization's sustainability in the next 3-5 years?
- How will the positive legacy of the leader be ensured?
- What are the key responsibilities and priorities the successor will need to focus on immediately?
- In helping the organization thrive, what are the essential responsibilities and relationships that will be important for the leader to share or to hand-off to staff before the successor arrives?
- How will the leader manage transitioning key relationships to the successor?

- What are the parameters for the leader to maintain key relationships on a personal and/or professional basis?
- If the leader, with the approval of the board, decides to maintain an ongoing relationship with the organization, how would she handle the changes that will emerge from new leadership?
- How can the board best support the leader through the transition planning process and through the transition?

Although clear and comprehensive transition planning can create a vision that allows the organization to see the forest through the trees, there is a huge distinction between a planned and an unplanned departure. To prepare for the sudden, unexpected departure of the founder/long-term leader an emergency transition plan should be adopted as soon as possible, incorporating the board, the founder and the senior staff members. This plan expands upon the existing succession plan, and:

- outlines the roles of senior staff and executive board leadership.
- provides a clear understanding of the critical leadership and management functions that will need to be filled.
- determines how decisions will be made on the operational issues required to ensure the sustainability of the organization.
- establishes if and how an interim executive will be identified.
- identifies the regular reporting processes and procedures that allow the board to closely monitor the implementation of the emergency plan.
- creates a transition planning committee to address acquiring permanent leadership.

Smooth, effective leadership transitions happen when thoughtful planning occurs and when the outgoing chief executive collaborates effectively with board leadership and the organization's senior leadership team in a transparent and inclusive way.

Even if a transition gets off on rocky footing, remember to "start where you are." Effective planning and processes can be put in place to redirect and ensure an effective transition to new leadership.

— Chapter 6 —
Reach for the Sky

While the pivotal moment of a leadership transition may start when the founder or long-term leader comes to the decision to depart, the thoughts of transition have probably been brewing long before that moment.

Some leaders burn out, and their decreased effectiveness over the course of months or years has become a burden to the organization. Others know they are ready to move on but are not able to do so because of financial considerations. Some are afraid to initiate a conversation with their boards because they fear being "walked out the door" earlier than they planned. On the other hand, board members may avoid initiating a conversation with the leader about succession, worrying that it could send the wrong message. While all of these concerns come from an emotional vantage point, they directly affect the very substance of the organization's operation and impact its day-to-day functioning.

One of the main factors that interferes with bringing this conversation to light is dependence on the leader. This dependence builds up over time because the organization has operated in the same fashion for many years and has become synonymous with the leader. It is difficult for board members, especially the ones that have long-term or close ties to the founder/leader, to visualize the continued success of the organization without that leader at the helm. They question how the organization could possibly be the same without the leader. And the truth is, it won't be. It is critical to the long-term success of the organization for the board to eliminate the dependence on a single leader and bring more people and more ideas into the mix before the leader's exit. This includes evaluating:

- mission and goals.
- supports and obstacles in the external environment.
- organizational structure and staff morale.
- programmatic and financial needs.
- constituency support.
- prior and future leadership requirements.

Not the Same

A leader, who was well known for being the face of her social service organization and working excessively long hours, remarked that no one on her staff would want to lead the organization and that she knew succession would be a struggle. In this particular case, it was clear that she was most likely right. No one would want to lead this organization *the way she led it*. It was equally clear that she felt her way was the only "right" way to lead. But there are many styles of leadership. This leader did not do a good job of delegating or cascading decision-making through her team. She was focused and passionate about the mission and the work, but she did not realize the value of devoting time or financial resources on developing leaders from within.

She saw no way to transition successfully. Clearly, she was unable to get out of her own way to see that someone else might do it differently, maybe even better. It did turn out to be a challenge to identify a successor, especially without an interim or transition plan.

A large national firm recruited and relocated a candidate to serve as her successor, but he departed after several months. The organization missed its opportunity for succession planning, and, unfortunately, the difficulty in finding a strong successor impacted the organization's reputation.

While each leader makes his unique contribution and can drive the success of an organization in a different way, the organization should still be free to develop when others take the lead.

The organization can begin to strengthen itself and lessen its dependence on the founder/ leader when it:

- increases key staff members' visibility by encouraging interaction with external partners and key stakeholders.
- creates a culture of transparency by sharing information and decision-making.
- promotes delegation by assessing the responsibilities of the founder or long-term leader and divvying up the tasks.
- focuses on ways to build capacity by expanding enterprising opportunities rather than cutting administrative costs.
- establishes two to three-year board terms with a strong succession plan, including mechanisms for the board to assess its performance.

Building the Arc: Crossing from Past to Future

"There is a difference between change and transition," according to William Bridges[8], a leading expert on organizational development. "Change is an *event*, such as when a leader departs and a new leader enters. *Transition* is much larger," writes Bridges, "and is defined by the complex emotional, psychological, and organizational shifts that occur while embracing that change."

Most people fear change. While the organization may address change on the operational level, it is often the emotional and psychological aspects of transition that challenge an organization's ability to effectively cope with change. Not all reactions to change are rational. Emotional reactions to change can be based on everything from how someone experienced change or flexibility as a child, to how comfortable he feels in his organizational role. That's why it is most important to take the pulse of the individuals involved in the organization to determine where they stand on change. While staff and board may accept that the world is in a continual state of flux, they often see a leadership transition as an interruption in their need for solid ground.

The change in leadership can be emotionally painful, especially when the loss is abrupt. While no two people will respond in the same way, the stages of grief do reflect a real sense of personal loss. For many

---

8 Bridges, William. Managing Transitions: Making the Most of Change, Perseus Printing, 2003.

Storm Cloud: Boards that are faced with replacing their chief executive typically turn first to the departing executive's job description. In actuality, that should be the last reference point for launching a search - because the old job description describes the leadership role of the organization of the past, not of the future.

individuals, the way that they respond to grief depends on how they have handled grief in their own lives.

Some individuals may feel a sense of abandonment or betrayal when a leader whom they trusted is no longer there for them. This can occur especially if they feel helpless and powerless. Denial, numbness, and shock can serve to protect the individual from experiencing the intensity of the loss. At times, individuals may ruminate about what could have been done to prevent the loss, blaming the organization and board leadership.

It is important to recognize the reality of these feelings. They seep in, despite the belief that we have compartmentalized our "business" selves from our "personal" selves. While expressing and accepting all feelings remains an important part of the change process, it is critical that these emotions are shared in a professional manner, and held within the parameters of benefitting rather than harming the organization.

Feelings of resentment may occur toward the next leader if the loss is not addressed. Facilitated groups can be established to allow a safe place and time to express thoughts and feelings regarding the loss, and to acknowledge and accept all feelings, both positive and negative. With room for those emotions, the staff can begin to acknowledge the change and start to see the opportunities inherent in the transition.

It becomes very important to address both the logistical and the emotional states of the organization. In a transition, organizations learn that by powering through change and moving into a positive place, they can own their resiliency, which, in turn, reduces the fear of change and allows change to be seen for the opportunity it is. An executive transition is a unique moment to shape the future of the organization, unconstrained by the prior executive's leadership capacity, capabilities, style or approach.

Instead of viewing this time as a crisis and rushing to find someone to take the reins immediately, organizations can positively experience this transition with the appointment of an interim executive director. This appointment generally takes place between the departure of the incumbent and the start of the new executive director. This *Interim Interlude* is one of the most overlooked opportunities in leadership transitions.

The Interim Interlude

Storm Cloud: The appointment of an internal staff or board member to the role of interim director is simply not as effective. It eliminates the power of the neutral opinion, potentially creating political tension, and does not give the organization an objective opportunity to assess its challenges to sustainability.

Providing stable management for an organization when it is without a permanent executive is certainly a crucial component, but so much more is possible. A well-trained interim can provide an active respite between a founder or other "big shoes" leader and a chosen successor. This interim time can be useful for the organization to come to terms with its history, address any latent issues, and for the staff, board members and volunteers to deal with their own sense of grief and loss as they prepare to embrace a new leader.

Having an interim executive director gives an organization a unique opportunity to engage in introspection and self-analysis while it searches for a permanent executive director. The intense work done by the organization during this period results in a much more accurate description of who the organization is, what it does, awareness of its strengths and challenges, and a shared vision of where it wants to go. As a result, hiring the right executive director becomes a more calculated, strategic and positive action, taken out of organizational strength, rather than a panicked reaction to organizational weakness.

Illumination: An interim leadership plan would allow the organization time to identify challenges and focus on the future. Too often, nonprofits rush to simply fill the leadership vacuum. It's hard to suggest slowing down the pace when the board is frenzied for a replacement.

An interim director can be extremely helpful during a planned, non-confrontational transition, and even more helpful if the transition was more sudden and negative with rancorous internal and external repercussions.

Ideally, the interim director will be an external appointment who will function both as the chief executive, leading the organization, and as a consultant, providing a neutral opinion on both process and substance for three to six months.

An externally hired interim director can help the board transition from founder or long-term leader to the new permanent successor by helping to:

- move the day-to-day operations forward.
- assess internal leadership talent at all levels of the organization.
- review organizational structure and recommend critical changes.
- maintain and improve organizational morale.
- evaluate financial stability, controls and management practices.
- analyze program strengths and weaknesses.
- provide guidance to the board.
- stabilize the agency's reputation to help attract qualified candidates for the executive director position.

The Perfect Storm, or How to Plan a Leadership Crisis

In Sebastian Junger's award winning novel, *The Perfect Storm*, a confluence of conditions combined to form a killer storm in the North Atlantic. The strong-willed and stubborn captain ignored the warnings and forged ahead, mortally endangering his crew and his ship. Leadership transitions can unleash the perfect storm organizationally in much the same way.

The perfect leadership storm often begins with denial. For many boards, it is just too painful to confront the thought that a beloved executive may need to, or choose to, move on. Whether the director is actively recruited away or faces a personal or family health crisis, the reality is that he or she at some point will leave. The harshest reality is that it sometimes happens on very short notice.

Part of this denial is also that the organization *believes* it will survive, regardless of difficult circumstances. It believes that because it does important work, funders will continue to support it through any crisis. Despite prevailing realities, boards often rely on the belief that stakeholders will rush to the rescue, throw out lifelines for important missions and save hemorrhaging organizations. Because of those beliefs, board members may not pay enough attention to their nonprofit's financial performance or its cash flow.

Another perfect storm condition is "untested assumptions," which are the second cousins to denial. The board *assumes* that the leader has built a strong infrastructure by hiring capable people and cultivating their leadership skills. Or they *assume* that board members have the skills to manage the interim leadership vacuum and at the same time lead the charge to hire a new executive director. But poorly managed executive transitions just make a bad situation worse, incurring high emotional and psychological costs for the organization and the communities it serves.

The Perfect Storm, or How to Plan a Leadership Crisis *continued*

To avoid the organization's perfect storm:

- assess leadership performance.
- focus attention on the organization's best and brightest so they don't jump ship.
- talk about succession planning as a natural part of strategic discussions.
- push for administrative support, infrastructure, or the expansion of the operations to ensure that appropriate, skilled talent is available.
- accept that board members or unprepared staff members cannot fill the leadership vacuum.
- evaluate optimal ways to conduct the search for a new executive director to reduce long-term emotional and psychological costs.
- fine tune the requirements for the next executive director.
- target communications about the vacancy.
- keep the organization's stakeholders informed.

Quite often, a change in executives will spotlight other needed changes in leadership, staffing, systems or structure, which are uncovered by the interim leadership. These changes can come in many forms. A disruptive board member might be encouraged to move on. A member of the management team who was loyal to the former chief executive may lack the interpersonal competencies to work in a collaborative setting. Or an organization may decide it needs to replace its underpowered financial system. A board can realize that its size is unwieldy and choose to downsize. One extreme example was a local service organization that faced a post-crisis loss of confidence and replaced its entire board because the old board was just too closely tied to the crisis.

One of the benefits of the interim executive director is to help the board come to terms with its own history by taking an unvarnished look at the organization and discerning its strengths, weaknesses, shortcomings, and accomplishments. When an organization is in crisis, especially if a termination was involved, there is often a tendency to magnify the shortcomings of the former leader while ignoring some of the underlying organizational issues that helped precipitate the crisis—issues that may have predated the executive's hiring and may well persist after she has left.

The interim director encourages the necessary changes to advance the organization while minimizing the disruption to the organization. For example, an interim may be faced with filling key staff vacancies. In that process, she could try to balance building a more effective staff with the need to preserve the latitude of a new executive's desire to build her own team.

The board can't hope to have a "solid platform" for a new executive if the foundation is wobbly because of unresolved underlying problems. Creating a solid foundation means ferreting out and addressing any problems as well as recognizing and truly appreciating the organization's strengths and accomplishments. In a crisis situation, there is usually such a rapid response to come to terms with the factors that precipitated the crisis that underlying issues are ignored. At the same time, the organization can leverage its strengths to resolve obstacles and put it back on a path to success.

Another foundation-building task that an interim can help with is to re-engage key stakeholders and supporters who may have drifted away. With an interim director who refocuses the mission and message, the leadership transition becomes a time to generate new excitement and find a successor who will match the forward motion of the organization.

All of this requires that an interim leader have sufficient time to prepare the organization for a more permanent leadership change. A parallel timeframe of three to six months also provides the necessary period for a comprehensive, well-structured search process.

Sometimes, hiring a new executive director takes longer than originally planned. This can occur for a variety of reasons but may be because the organization is perceived by external stakeholders to be in disarray. An interim director can strengthen the organization, clarify the position, and make the job more desirable for prospective candidates.

Some boards worry that using the interim approach can have negative repercussions with funders and donors, jeopardizing promised financial resources. While in the past some funders have delayed grants during a leadership transition, the board can mitigate this possibility in several ways. First, when it's clear that the board has engaged in careful succession and transition planning, and the interim appointment is a part of that, funders are less concerned about the organization's ability to function effectively between permanent chief executives, and will view the appointment as a positive proactive and strategic step. Second, regular communication throughout this time is another critical tool in developing the confidence of funders, donors and other key stakeholders. A communication plan that delineates who is responsible for communication with various stakeholders is an important component of any succession plan.

The final step of the interim process is for the board and the staff to truly commit to the new permanent executive and the new direction. The opportunity for the board is to look forward, explore what the organization can be, and then shape the job and the job description around the present and future leadership needs.

At this point, the organization should have a healthy perspective on its history, have built a solid platform for the new executive, and have a clear sense of the organizational direction and key priorities. In short, the organization should be prepared to launch and support its new leader with a defined and clear direction.

Selecting the Right Executive

Typically, boards focus solely on the executive search as the all-important activity. The essence of a successful executive transition is to broaden the thinking beyond "just recruitment" to embrace the entire succession planning-organizational assessment-leadership change continuum.

Selecting the chief executive is the board's most significant decision. It is important to take great care in the search for a new director, determine compensation, and establish responsibilities and accountability to the board.

The selection process should begin with an organizational assessment to determine the desired skills, competencies and leadership profile for the new chief executive. Once an organizational assessment has been completed, the next step involves forming a search committee that will manage the entire recruiting process on behalf of the board. It is advisable to invite key staff members to also take part in the final interviews and to provide input to the search committee during the selection process.

Additionally, the role of the departing founder/leader during and following the transition should be clearly defined with his or her role in the search process limited.

The Search Committee

The Search Committee moves the search from a prospective pool of candidates to a final recommendation. The board, to whom the new executive will report, confirms the recommended candidate and extends the offer. The specific responsibilities of the search committee are to:

- create the timeframe and specific deadlines for the search process.
- prepare a budget, including the costs of consulting services and travel for candidates.
- promote the position in their networks.

- act as a conduit between the organization and its constituencies on the progress of the search.
- identify and interview semi-finalists based on criteria set out in the position description.
- prioritize selected finalists and thoroughly assess their competencies and fit, including the completion of due diligence such as reference checking.
- select the finalist and make the recommendation to the full board for approval.
- create the terms of the offer and negotiate compensation package with the successful candidate.
- orient the new hire and facilitate the transition through the first six months.

Depending on the organization's size, complexity and resources, some boards choose to use an executive search firm. The selection of a search firm should include an assessment of the firm's ability to determine the candidate with the best cultural fit. Whether the organization chooses a boutique or national firm, it is critical in determining a successful fit that the search consultants are able to effectively assess the leadership needs and provide examples of their ability to guide a search committee through candidate selection and integration. A knowledgeable search firm can tap into an extensive network of potential candidates from their own database as well as through effective targeting of relevant programs or service-driven organizations.

If an outside search firm is not used, a staff coordinator is essential to help the search committee manage the logistics of the search, create candidate files, respond to applicants, and organize the committee meetings. Choose the staff coordinator wisely. He or she must be capable of maintaining complete confidentiality and not share details of the search inappropriately with other staff.

Whether a search firm is hired or the entire process is handled internally, the steps for effective executive recruitment are the same. The effort includes the ability to:

- identify leadership competencies and the experience required in the new leader.
- conduct a comprehensive search for candidates who meet the leadership criteria.
- assess all internal prospects based on the leadership criteria.
- identify and evaluate all prospective candidates using consistent behavioral interview questions and scenarios.
- guide the organization through the interview and selection process.
- complete comprehensive referencing for all finalist candidates.
- ensure a smooth executive on-boarding/integration process.

Specific criteria need to be established with regard to the competencies, characteristics and qualifications that the board considers most desirable in the chief executive. The measures of leadership competence will be reflected in the education and experience of the candidate as well as specific industry and practical skills required for the job.

There are also personal characteristics, such as emotional intelligence and the ability to engage in difficult conversations, and values that are known to serve leaders positively. It is important to consider and be able to evaluate those values that will contribute to a potential candidate's success. Defining these specifics prior to seeing candidates allows the search committee to create clear criteria before getting into an analysis of personalities. Once the search committee focuses on particular candidates, it becomes more difficult to be objective.

The search committee (in conjunction with a search firm or consultant, if one is retained) develops a position description, which highlights what the board expects the chief executive to accomplish, how the position relates to the board, and elaborates on the specific tasks and responsibilities.

Prior to the start of any interviews, the search committee should obtain the board's approval for the position description. They should also gain acceptance for the recommended criteria, competencies, experience and qualifications that they consider most desirable for the chief executive.

Storm Cloud: To determine the best candidates, it is critical to inform serious contenders of the realities of the organization's present situation. Any serious issues, such as the financial condition, prospective funding, or adequacy of staffing levels, need to be disclosed to the leading candidates before a final hiring decision is made. The response of the candidates to both the challenges and opportunities becomes an important consideration for both parties.

The best way to identify good prospects is to contact a broad group of people and start to build a list of candidates. Most qualified chief executives do not apply directly for jobs. Instead, they are often invited and encouraged to apply. It is important to continue to disseminate information into outer circles of the organization's network as a key step in learning who is "out there."

Additionally, it is important to the integrity of the relationship that the new chief executive fully comprehends the organization's situation, rather than feeling misled later. Organizations risk losing their top candidate if they try to hide the facts, which the new chief executive will uncover once they assume the role.

Because the role of the chief executive is so central to the success of the organization, those charged with the hiring process must be prepared to negotiate adequate compensation and consider incentives to attract a highly desirable candidate. Care should be taken in presenting a written offer, after the verbal offer is made.

A comprehensive executive search process includes successful candidate selection, as well as coaching to integrate the new chief executive into the organization and with the board. Once hired, the board chair and a senior staff member should help ease the new chief executive through the transition period. How the board and staff begin building their professional relationships during this stage has a lot to do with the new leader's long-term success.

Chapter 7: Smooth Sailing
Thoughtful On-Boarding: Ensuring Success of the Leadership Hire

Leadership transitions require attention and support. The attention paid by the board chair and the chief executive in developing their professional relationship during the first three to six months will have a lot to do with the organization's and the new leader's long-term success. The board can adopt a thriving leadership practice by assuming responsibility for the integration of the new chief executive into the organization. This is defined as on-boarding.

The selection of the hire is a critical point in the leadership transition, but the integration and goal setting with the new executive will determine the success of the transition. A smooth and timely integration will assure his or her success and accelerate the ability to have an immediate impact with positive results. The first 90 days are the most critical to the assimilation of the new executive.

Retaining an executive coach to work with the newly-hired leader can be useful. In some cases, the board chair will also benefit from external leadership coaching to effectively support the new chief executive and to lead the board through transition. In some cases, the board chair will benefit from external leadership coaching to effectively support the new chief executive and to lead the board through the transition. Embarking on a productive relationship with the new chief executive enables the board, and especially the chair, to show support for the organization's future direction. The board should maintain responsibility for governance, while remaining appropriately detached from daily operations. It is also essential to establish the lines and methods of communication between board and staff.

The on-boarding process includes clearly defined goals and expectations for the first six months. To support the optimum transition, the board should also consider performance-based incentives and conversations with the new executive director to specifically address any rational and emotional reactions that surface relative to the transition through team building and change management initiatives.

Another critical factor in supporting the new executive is to maintain or extend the tenure of the current board chair. Two parallel leadership changes can be destabilizing for the professional and volunteer leadership.

The board can adopt a thriving leadership practice by assuming responsibility for the integration of the new chief executive into the stakeholder community. To do this, the board should first engage in its own appraisal process to ensure its commitment to growth and governance, and then provide continuous opportunities and introductions to current and potential donors and funders. When the board embarks on a productive relationship with the new chief executive, the entire board, and especially the chair, supports the organization's future direction, maintains responsibility for governance, and remains appropriately uninvolved in daily operations.

To maximize the chief executive's transition, it is critical for the board and the new leader to establish clear goals and expectations for the first six months. To achieve those goals and expectations, the chief executive should be encouraged to define clear lines of ongoing communication with and between the board and staff.

A focused on-boarding process can enhance the integration and assimilation of the chief executive because it:

- accelerates the staff and the leader's learning curves so the tone and style of the new executive director can be quickly matched to the role, informed by the new culture.
- defines joint expectations and measurable goals in the partnership between board chair and chief executive.
- develops introductions and opportunities for collaborative relationships with key stakeholders.

- allows for a robust understanding of others' organizational points of view.
- clarifies the "formal" and "informal" decision-making power in the organization.

It is important to celebrate the transition by creating an opportunity to publicly honor the outgoing leader and introduce the new CEO to all the organization's stakeholders.

A public "pass the torch" event will acknowledge the contributions of the outgoing leader and give him or her the deserved honor for ushering the organization to that moment in time. This public event also provides a new beginning for the successor with introductions to all the key stakeholders in the immediate and larger community.

The selection of the hire is a critical point in the process, but the integration and goal setting with the new executive will determine the success of the transition. A smooth and timely integration will assure her success and accelerate her ability to have an immediate impact with positive results.

Illumination: The first 90 days are critical to the assimilation of the new executive. Determine who on the board will take responsibility for this onboarding process.

— Chapter 8 —
Moving Forward

One of the most important aspects of organizational life is to recognize that change is a constant. Good leaders have the vision and detail focus to execute on the organization's growth and sustainability. It is important to be aware that as the environment continues to change, resources will become more abundant or scarce, needs will evolve, and similar organizations will develop with whom the organization can partner, merge, compete, or ignore.

The responsibility of every organization is to be prepared for change through a realistic and timely assessment of where it stands now, where it wants to be now, and where it wants to be in the future.

Leadership change offers a moment of rare opportunity. It is a time to gain perspective on the organization and to bring in talent that supports and positions the organization to be even stronger moving forward. That is, most simply, the goal: to use the energy and strengths of the leadership of senior staff and the board to bring the organization to a point where it truly serves its mission in a way that also optimizes personal growth and development for the people involved.

Leading change is important work. "Speed of change is the driving force. Leading change competently is the only answer," according to John Kotter, *Leading Change*[9] .

Just as we think we have come to that moment in time where we can stop and take a breath, change offers us another opportunity for a different way, a different perspective. We are always ending and always beginning. And the best perspective we can hold is to know that the journey is all there is. Truth be told, we never actually get there. And the bigger truth is that there is no "there" to be gotten. Enjoy the ride.

---

9 Kotter, John. "Leading Change," Harvard Business Review Press, 2012.

Four Stages of Change™
── Stage I: Resistance ──

Primary Issues

- Awareness
- Desire
- Loss
- Anger
- Insecurity
- Shock
- Powerlessness
- Valued people leave

Observable Behaviors

- Sadness
- Withdrawal
- Cautiousness
- Anger
- Sarcasm
- Apathy
- Resentment
- Rumors/speculation
- Verbal/written animosity internally/externally

Costs to the Organization

- Decreased productivity
- No creativity and risk taking
- Increased absenteeism
- Sabotage
- Time and energy go into rumors and speculation hurting organization's reputation
- Loss of talent
- Diminished credibility/ trust/influence

Outcomes

- An awareness of the need for the change
- A communication plan
- Consistent, timely messages
- Work environment that allows for resistance to be expressed openly
- Frequent communication using multiple approaches

Specific Leadership Actions

- Identify barriers of awareness and desire to change
- Listen carefully
- Make the change safe for discussion
- Accept employees' reactions
- Hold frequent meetings
- Create opportunities for involvement
- Be visible
- Maintain lines of communication
- Make certain information is current and consistent
- Offer support and reassurance
- Keep employees accountable for day-to-day results
- TELL THE TRUTH

Four Stages of Change™
Stage II: Confusion

Primary Issues

- Knowledge
- Ability
- Credibility
- Focus
- Clarity
- Tenuous relationships
- Unclear roles/ responsibilities

Observable Behaviors

- Questions, questions and more questions
- Grumbling and complaining
- Lack of cooperation
- Escalation of political behavior
- Frustration
- Erratic performance
- Skepticism
- Reluctance to be accountable
- Making assumptions
- Poor listening

Costs to the Organization

- False starts
- Duplication of effort
- Decline in quality
- Poor working relationships
- Competitors take advantage and openly go after talent and customers

Outcomes

- Clarification of goals
- Redefinition of individual roles and responsibilities
- Formation of work teams
- Review of priorities, expectations and accountabilities
- Identification of training needs
- Initiation of training programs

Specific Leadership Actions

- Provide answers, answers and more answers
- Repeat key information often
- Restate goals and priorities
- Spell out roles/ responsibilities in detail
- Set short-term goals
- Make sure customer needs are met
- Maintain standards; hold employees accountable
- Create opportunities for participation
- Hold meetings for planning and problem solving
- Stay approachable
- Conduct individual coaching sessions
- Create incentives for high performers
- Identify crtical knowledge and skills needs
- Get employees trained

Four Stages of Change™
Stage III: Integration

Primary Issues

- Testing
- Recognition
- Stability
- Bargaining
- Renewal

Observable Behaviors

- Renewed energy
- Excitement
- Optimism
- Independence
- Willingness to take small risks
- Interest in team participation
- Confidence restored
- Improved productivity

Costs to the Organization

- Exaggerated budgets
- Unrealistic goals/prorities
- Loss of focus
- Things fall through the cracks
- Overstaffing

Outcomes

- Recognition of people's efforts
- Clearly defined priorities/ deadlines
- Stabilized work environment
- Effectively functioning work teams
- Improved levels of productivity
- Implementation of professional development plans

Specific Leadership Actions

- Encourage employees to identify and recommend improvements to work flow
- Establish policies, procedures and processes
- Keep communication robust and value-added
- Make certain goals are reasonable/achievable
- Prepare professional development plans
- Celebrate milestones
- Continue to keep employees focused
- Offer ongoing, constructive feedback
- Provide individual coaching

Four Stages of Change™
Stage IV: Commitment

Primary Issues

- Reinforcement
- Empowerment
- Flexibility
- Productivity
- Future opportunities

Observable Behaviors

- Action oriented
- Open expression of differences
- High energy
- Personal satisfaction
- Willingness to take risks
- Team interdependence
- Verbal/written support of the company

Costs to the Organization

- Complacency
- Inattention to new trends/ environment
- Self-satisfaction
- Everyone in agreement (groupthink mentality)
- Unprepared for the next change(s)

Outcomes

- Customer needs close monitoring
- High levels of performance
- Job enrichment and satisfaction
- Employees flexible and ready for the next change(s)

Specific Leadership Actions

- Foster customer loyalty
- Pay attention to trends/external environment
- Keep generating new ideas
- Engage in team building initiatives
- Stimulate participation and involvement
- Reward high performance
- Continue to celebrate milestones
- Encourage outcome thinking
- Find best ways to sustain the change effort

Short-Term Emergency Succession Plan

Succession Plan in the Event of a Temporary, Unplanned Absence:
A temporary absence is defined as one of less than four months in which the anticipation is that the chief executive (or key manager) will return to his/her position once the situation that precipitated the absence is resolved.

As soon as the circumstances occur, there should be communications with board leadership and an emergency leadership plan should be created. This document would clarify the leader's key responsibilities and identify who could perform those responsibilities. In some cases, this would also require a plan to build up the skills of those individuals. This emergency leadership plan should:

- Identify the current critical leadership and management functions of the chief executive.
- Determine who will take responsibility for managing the organization or aspects of the organization and what authority and compensation will be afforded to that individual(s).
- Determine if and how an acting chief executive should be appointed.
- Determine who on the board will provide oversight to the acting ED or other person(s) managing day-to-day operations in the absence of the chief executive.
- Enact a pre-determined communications plan to inform staff, board and stakeholders of the temporary leadership structure.
- Draft a communications plan to be implemented if an emergency succession occurs.

Emergency Succession Planning Questions
For a Temporary, Unplanned Absence

- How does the organization define a temporary absence?
- Which board committee(s) will manage the emergency succession process? (Executive? Governance? An appointed ad hoc committee?)
- Who is designated to assume leadership the in the absence of the chief executive? What authority will they have?
- What process will you use to contact and inform staff when an unplanned absence occurs?
- Who will communicate with stakeholders? When and how?
- How will staff engage in managing in the absence of the chief executive?
    - How will the chief executive's portfolio of work be managed?
    - What projects and activities can be delayed temporarily?
    - Do the designated staff possess the essential capabilities to take on the leadership responsibilities?
    - How will you backfill and support current staff who may need to take on some of the CEO tasks and responsibilities?
    - Are there board members available who can volunteer to assist with some of the necessary tasks?
- Who on the board will provide oversight to the individual(s) who are tasked with leading the organization in the absence of the chief executive?
- What process will be put in place to re-integrate the chief executive into the organization when he or she is ready to return?
- If a temporary absence continues longer than anticipated, what adjustments to the initial process or plan will need to occur? Who will take responsibility to manage that process?

Transition Succession Planning Questions
For the Permanent Departure of the CEO

- Which board committee will manage the transition of the permanent departure of the chief executive?
- How will you communicate the departure of the CEO, and the subsequent process for managing the interim period, and selecting the successor?
- Should you consider hiring an interim executive?
- How will you keep staff and stakeholders informed about the search process?
- How will you determine the process for conducting a search for a new chief executive? Will you need to consider using an outside search consultant for all or part of the search process?
- How will you communicate with staff and board throughout the search process?
- What assistance might the staff need to manage through a change in leadership?
- What, if any, type of "good-bye" celebration is needed to thank the departing chief executive? Will this event be linked to the introduction of the new chief executive to smooth the transition?
- How will you support the new CEO during his or her first 30, 60 and 90 days? Who on the board will take responsibility for this "onboarding" process?

Index

Endorsements

"Great leaders have the power to transform organizations. And with the change brought about by the inevitable departure of these leaders, their organizations, staff and boards can be thrust into a state of panic and fear. In their new book, Priscilla Rosenwald and Lesley Mallow Wendell bring to life how to bridge this gap effectively through honest reflection and thoughtful planning. At once strategic and approachable, *When Leaders Leave* is a comprehensive resource, replete with examples, gauges and guides, that nonprofit CEOs and board members alike will benefit from immensely by adding to their toolkits."
Jennifer Buffett
President, NoVo Foundation

"As a funder, we're constantly asking nonprofit boards to tell us about their succession planning. It's pretty rare to get an answer. Priscilla Rosenwald and Lesley Wendell are seasoned professionals with extensive experience helping organizations plan and execute successful leadership transitions. This book gives boards and CEOs tools to deal comfortably with the challenges and opportunities inherent in these transitions."
Kevin Murphy
President, Berks County Community Foundation and
Former Board Chair, Council on Foundations

"When Leaders Leave is timely and important. Rosenwald and Wendell focus on the transformational forces that transitions produce and then provide the guidance organizational leaders need to make sure those forces produce good results. In the CDFI industry, where a generational leadership change is underway, When Leaders Leave can be a valuable resource."
Mark Pinsky
President & CEO, Opportunity Finance Network

"Take the time to read this! Being prepared for inevitable transition is one of the most important responsibilities for leadership in assuring a stable and healthy future of an organization. Lesley and Priscilla lay out the issues clearly here and provide a roadmap for thinking about what is required, and more importantly what is inevitable. Take the time to read this. Take the time to seriously use its road map. It is one of the greatest gifts you can give to your organization and its future."
Martin Cohen
Partner, The Cultural Planning Group

"Great read for Executives and Board members. Leadership development, retention and succession should be part of regular board and agency discussions."
Cynthia F. Figueroa
CEO, Congreso

"This is a useful primer on preparing for leadership change and is especially relevant for funders who have grantees facing an executive transition. It is full of relevant anecdotes and straightforward, clear advice for organizations, boards and leaders alike."
Ronna Brown
President, Philanthropy New York

"We've been hearing about leadership transition issues for the past several years. We now know that nonprofits all around the country are facing the impending transition of their "baby boomer" leaders retiring and bringing on the next generation of leadership. Smooth transitions are key for these mission-driven organizations.

The leadership transitions need to be carefully planned between boards and these long-time leaders if they are to go smoothly. This book is among the first that clearly and succinctly outlines the issues and options for how these transitions can be smoothly navigated. If you are a board member, a CEO, or someone who has a stake in these leadership transitions, this book will be enormously helpful to you."
Eileen R. Heisman
President and CEO, National Philanthropic Trust

About the Authors

TransitionWorks helps organizations cultivate the resilience and the agility to thrive by developing and implementing ongoing leadership legacy planning. Priscilla Rosenwald and Lesley Mallow Wendell help nonprofit CEOs and board chairs prepare for current and potential change. Their combined experiences have given them a bird's eye view of the trials and tribulations organizations face in finding and growing high quality talent who align with the goals of the organization. Together they have facilitated ongoing Nonprofit CEO Roundtables focused on leadership transition, have authored numerous articles and speak frequently on leadership development and organizational effectiveness.

Priscilla Rosenwald
Founder/Principal, Leadership Recruiters

Across the country, clients in the nonprofit and corporate sectors have turned to Priscilla for organizational consulting, executive hiring and talent management. She is highly distinguished in the search industry, presenting her clients with the rare combination of both management and recruiting experience. Priscilla has an enhanced ability to align nonprofits and social innovation companies' management and cultural priorities with candidate assessment and placement to ensure organizational success.

Before establishing Leadership Recruiters, Priscilla was a principal of HealthLink, a consulting firm specializing in board development, strategic planning and project management for non-profit organizations. She has been a member of the senior management teams of corporate and non-profit healthcare and service organizations, leading project management and national training collaborations. She also worked as an Executive Recruiter with Heidrick & Struggles, Inc., where she placed chief executives and board members in a wide range of organizations.

Priscilla serves as a frequent keynote speaker to professional organizations on leadership change, transitioning from the for-profit sector and board recruitment. She serves on professional and cultural boards, and holds a Masters degree from Hunter College in Group and Organizational Development and a Bachelors degree from Temple University.

Lesley Mallow Wendell
Founder/Principal, Rosewood Consulting Group

Lesley works with entrepreneurs and nonprofit leaders to increase their ability to motivate their teams and improve overall performance and productivity through executive coaching, organizational effectiveness, and leadership development programs. She also facilitates strategic planning processes and leadership retreats.

Prior to establishing Rosewood Consulting Group in 2001, Lesley served as the chief executive of a Philadelphia-based career and human resource consulting organization and held previous positions in advertising and academia. In addition to her organizational work, Lesley served as an adjunct faculty member of the Management Department at Cedar Crest College. She also served as Director of Career Services at Widener University where she created a comprehensive counseling and recruiting center for undergraduate and graduate students.

Lesley continues to serve in various professional and community associations. In 2008, the Women Presidents' Organization selected Lesley to chair its Philadelphia Chapter where she continues to facilitate a monthly roundtable for women entrepreneurs who head multi-million dollar companies.

She has been a keynote speaker for many professional organizations and has provided expert opinion in local and national publications and broadcast media focused on the topic of leadership development. Lesley earned an M.S. in Human Resource Management from Widener University and an undergraduate degree, granted cum laude, from the University of Pennsylvania.